TIM JEFFS ART
Animal Sketches
ENDANGERED Baby ANIMALS

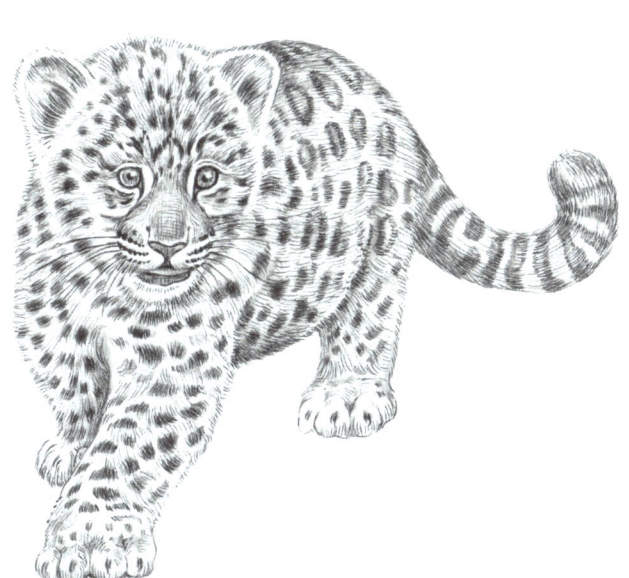

A Special Edition Coloring Book

For Jane, Jenna and Harrison

Dedicated to all of the wonderful colorists who have supported my art and made my drawings more beautiful with their colors, and all the precious creatures that we live among.
A special thank you to Jo Warren for all of her continued support and beautiful colorings and lesson that make this book so much more special!

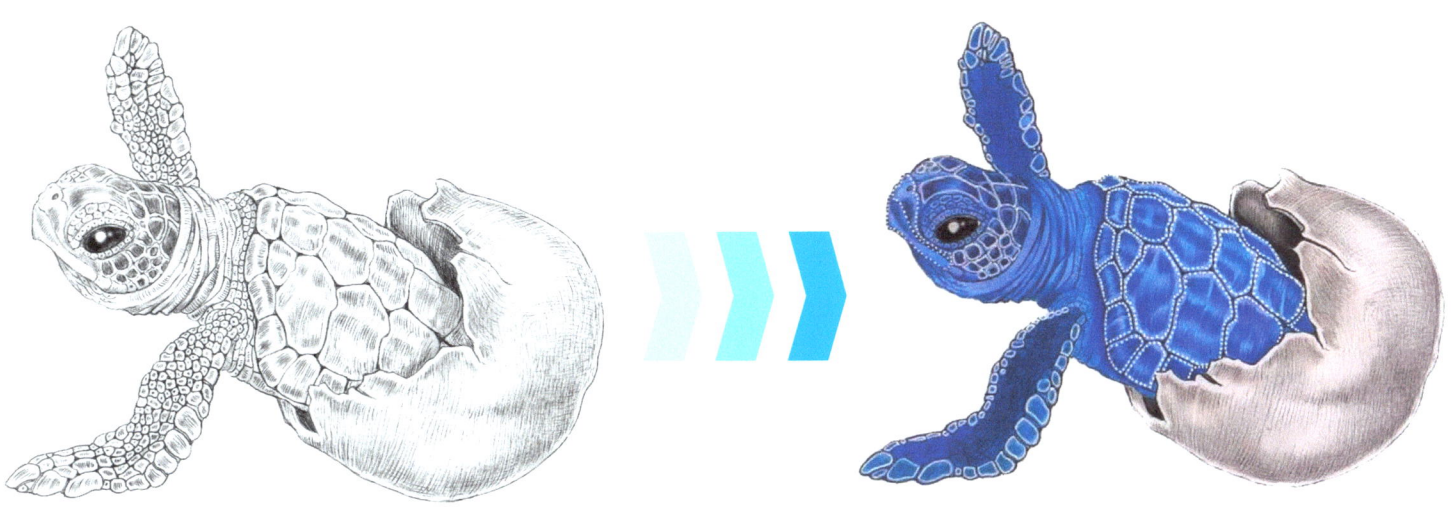

© Copyright 2021 Tim Jeffs Art
All rights reserved. No part of this publication may be reproduced or distributed in any form without the prior written permission of Tim Jeffs Art.

Tim Jeffs Art
376 East Madison Avenue, Dumont, NJ 07628

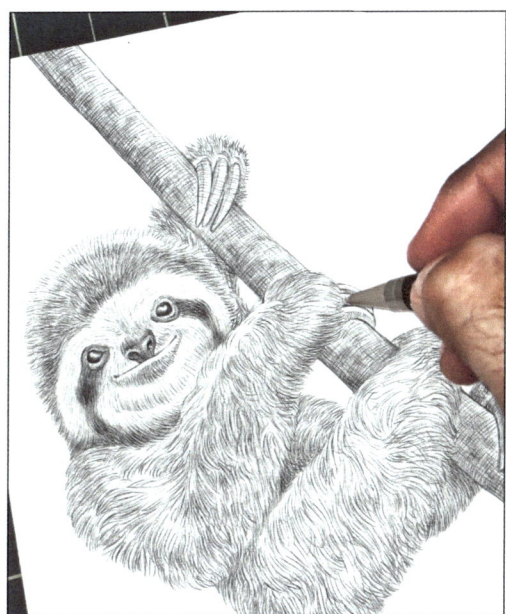 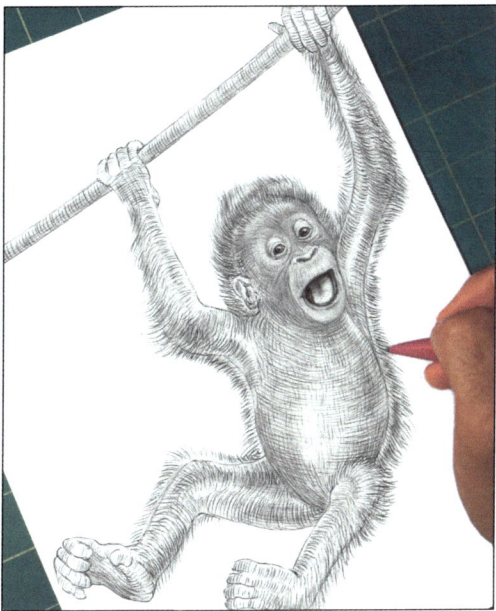 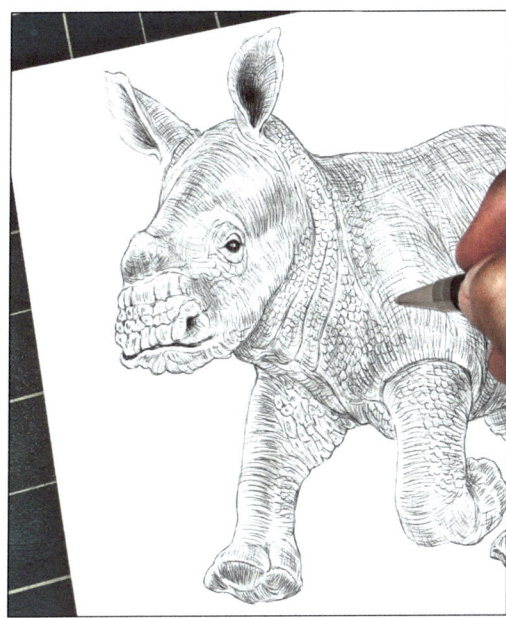

Endangered Baby Animal Sketches Thoughts

Who can resist baby animals? Not me! Their playful mannerisms are irresistible to watch and even more fun to create drawings of. Baby animals warm our hearts when we see them. They make us smile and laugh. They are the next generation who give us hope that animals will continue to thrive and prosper.

It was a goal of mine to create a coloring book that focused on endangered baby animals for two reasons. The first being an overwhelming request from colorists for a coloring book of baby animal drawings. And the second is my hope to continue to raise awareness of endangered animals. The animals that are struggling to survive need our utmost attention, and baby animals are the best ambassadors of this cause!

I hope you enjoy coloring this group of endangered baby animal sketches as much as I enjoyed drawing them, and I know that with your colors, you will bring them running, playing, and climbing to life! Have fun!

GRAYSCALE COLORING LESSON
Pygmy three-toed sloth

Lesson level: Easy

Coloring the
Pygmy Three-Toed Sloth

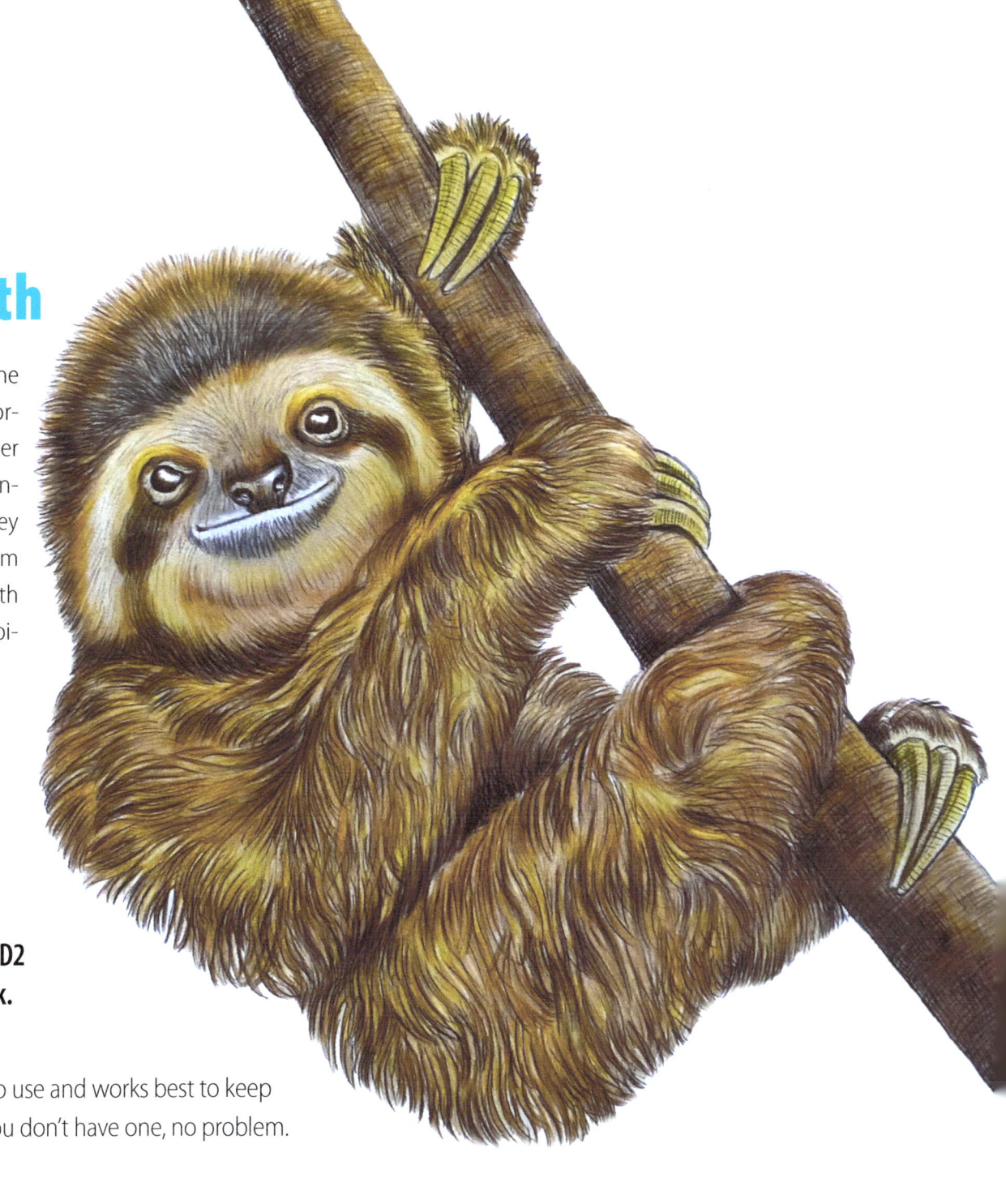

On the next page I will walk you through the coloring of the Pygmy three-toed sloth baby which is on page 11 of this coloring book. These adorable sloths are much smaller than the other 3 members of its genus and live on an island off the cost of Panama. Sloths have a very special place in my heart because they are my daughter Jenna's favorite animal, and when I draw them they make me think of her. This beautiful coloring of the Sloth was done by Jo Warren. Many thanks for her creative and inspirational step-by-step photos in the coloring lesson.

❱ Supply List

In this lesson, Tombow Colored Pencils were used, (pencil numbers listed below) but you can use any brand with similar colors.

1) **The coloring page can be found on page 11**
2) **Colors: Tombow Irojiten: LG 3 Sallow, P10 Pigeon Gray, D2 Chestnut Brown, DL2 Cinnamon Brown, V10 Ivory Black. Tombow 1500: #32 Dark Brown**
3) **Pencil Sharpener:** An electric pencils sharpener is easy to use and works best to keep your pencils extra sharp and your hand less sore. But if you don't have one, no problem. A hand pencil sharpener works just fine too.

GRAYSCALE COLORING LESSON
Pygmy three-toed sloth

Pygmy Three-Toed Sloth

Supplies needed: 6 colored pencils

Coloring Steps by Jo Warren

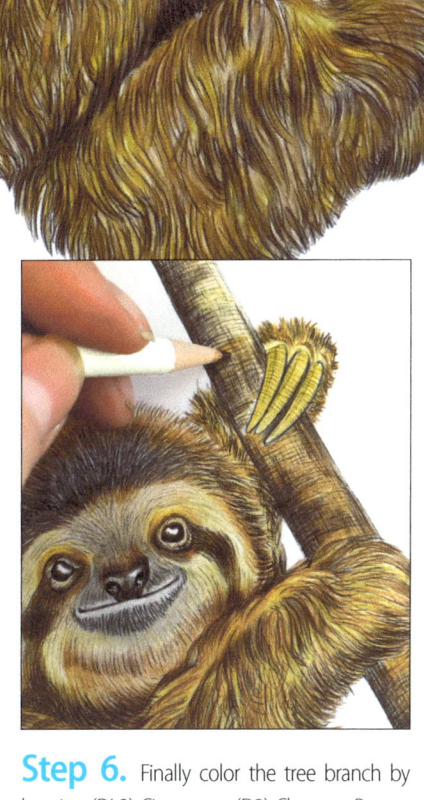

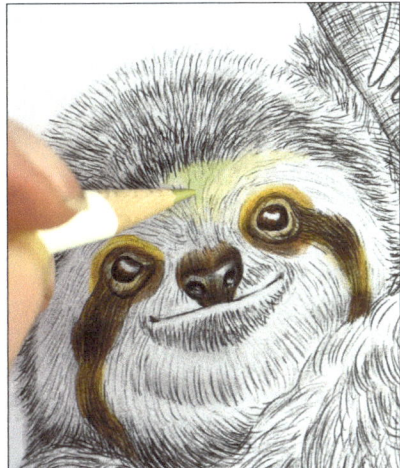

Step 1. Color (DL2) Cinnamon Brown around the eyes and dark face fur.. Layer (D2) Chestnut Brown over parts of the same area and eyeballs. Add a base layer of (LG3) Sallow on the face.

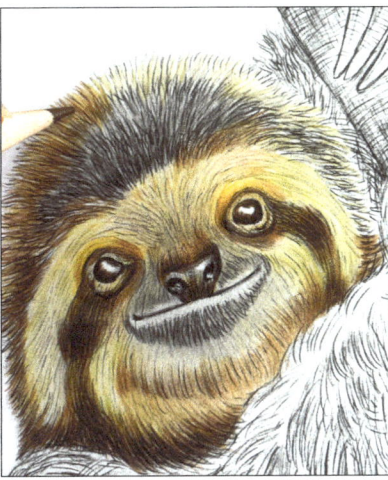

Step 2. Color a light layer of (DL2) Cinnamon over the face. Around the mouth, nose and top of the head color (P10) Pigeon Gray and blend (D2) Chestnut Brown into the edge of the gray area.

**You did it!
Your endangered Pygmy three-toed sloth is done!**

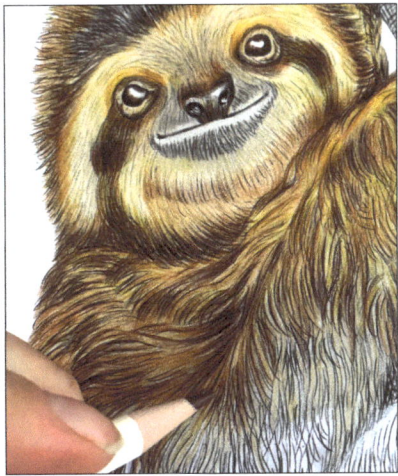

Step 3. The key to creating thick fur is layering your colors from light to dark. Build up your color by coloring lines that follow the hairs in the drawings rather then filling in a whole area with color.

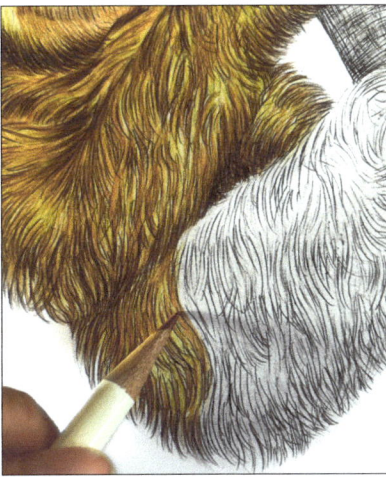

Step 4. For the fur use this sequence of colors. Start with (LG3) Sallow, then (DL2) Cinnamon, (D2) Chestnut Brown, (#32) Dark Brown, and finally streaks of (V10) Ivory Black.

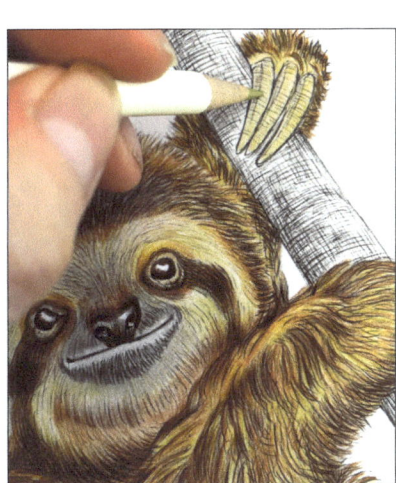

Step 5 Color the sloths claws with a combination of (LG3) Sallow and (P10) Pigeon Gray. Outline the claws with (V10) Ivory Black to give them a sharp edge.

Step 6. Finally color the tree branch by layering (DL2) Cinnamon, (D2) Chestnut Brown, and (#32) Dark Brown on the other edges to give the branch a three dimensional look.

Spreading Awareness through Coloring

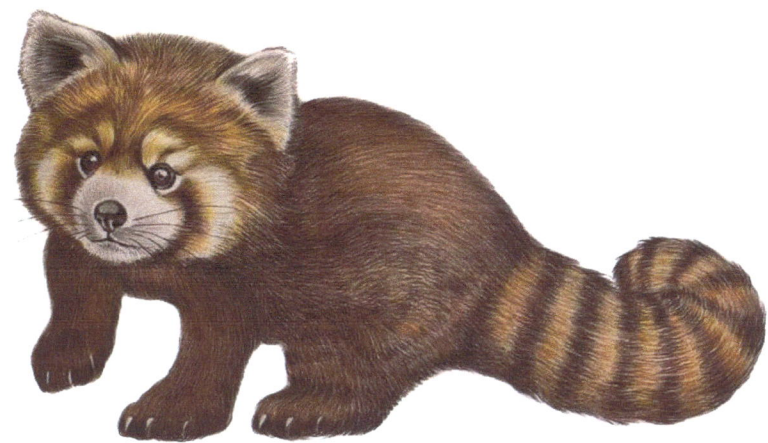

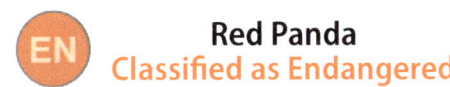

Red Panda
Classified as Endangered

I truly believe that raising awareness through the sharing of my artwork is a fantastic way to educate people about conservation. And coloring animals is a beautiful way to learn about them as you enjoy a relaxing and fun pastime. On the following page, I listed the baby animals statuses on the *International Union for Conservation of Nature's (IUCN)* conservation list. I think it's important to include the *(IUCN)* conservation list so people understand the classifications more clearly. To the right is an overview of the IUCN's conservation list, which breaks animals' conservation statuses into several categories. Knowing what these categories mean and the animals that are included in them is extremely important. **Together through art we can change the world!**

Tim Jeffs
Animal Artist

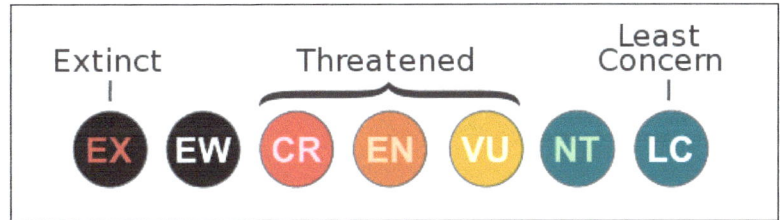

The list consists of 7 categories. From Least Concerned all the way to Extinct. Here are the definitions of each category:

- **LEAST CONCERN (LC):** A species that has been evaluated but not qualified for any other category on the list.
- **NEAR THREATENED (NT):** A species that may be considered threatened with extinction in the near future.
- **VULNERABLE (VU):** A species likely to become endangered unless the circumstances that are threatening its survival and reproduction improve.
- **ENDANGERED (EN):** A species that is considered very likely to become extinct.
- **CRITICALLY ENDANGERED (CR):** A species that is facing an extremely high risk of becoming extinct in the wild.
- **EXTINCT IN THE WILD (EW):** A species that is only known by living members kept in captivity or as a naturalized population outside its historic range due to massive habitat loss.
- **EXTINCT (EX):** A species that has been terminated.

Learn about the Endangered Baby Animals

Before you start coloring, it's important to learn where the baby animals in this book live and know why they are considered endangered.

❯ Amur Leopard
With fewer than 60 individuals estimated to survive in Russia and China it is considered as one of the rarest cats on Earth.
Conservation Status: Critically Endangered

❯ Asiatic Cheetah
Confined to central Iran, as of 2016, only 43 individuals were estimated to survive.
Conservation Status: Critically Endangered

❯ Black Rhinoceros
Around 1900 there were probably several hundred thousand living in Africa, but by 2004 only 2400 remained. In 2019 the population was 5,500 and was either steady or slowly increasing.
Conservation Status: Critically Endangered

❯ Borneo Pygmy Elephant
There are only an estimated 1,500 individuals remaining in the wild. The primary threat to these elephants is habitat loss
Conservation Status: Endangered

❯ Columbia Basin Pygmy Rabbit
Considered the smallest North American rabbit and confined to the Columbia Basin in Central Washington state there are less than 30 believed to live in the wild.
Conservation Status: Endangered

❯ Giant Panda
Thankfully with conservation efforts the Giant Panda populations have been increasing. Scientists believe the wild population may be as large as 3,000
Conservation Status: Endangered (ESA)

❯ Green Sea Turtle
The primary threats facing green turtles are by catch in commercial and recreational fishing gear. Populations are estimated at 85-90 thousand nesting females
Conservation Status: Endangered

❯ Mountain Gorilla
Conservation efforts have led to an increase in numbers and the overall population is now believed to be at over 1,000 individuals.
Conservation Status: Endangered

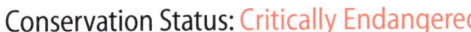

❯ Northern Rockhopper Penguins
The current population is estimated to be between 100,000–499,999 breeding pairs, compared to millions in the 1950s.
Conservation Status: Endangered

❯ Polar Bear
Threatened by global warming and loss of sea ice the global population of polar bears is between 22,000 to 31,000 individuals.
Conservation Status: Endangered (ESA)

❯ Pygmy Three-Toed Sloth
Significantly smaller than the other three members of its genus, in 2012 the total population was estimated at only 79.
Conservation Status: Critically Endangered

❯ Red Panda
The wild population is estimated at fewer than 10,000 mature individuals and continues to decline due to habitat loss.
Conservation Status: Endangered

❯ Ring-Tailed Lemur
Due to habitat destruction only about 2,000 ring-tailed lemurs are estimated to be left in the wild.
Conservation Status: Endangered

❯ South China Tiger
Possibly extinct in the wild since no wild individual has been recorded since the late 1980s.
Conservation Status: Critically Endangered

❯ Sumatran Orangutan
Fewer than 14,000 Sumatran orangutans remain In the wild.
Conservation Status: Critically Endangered

Baby Animals Index

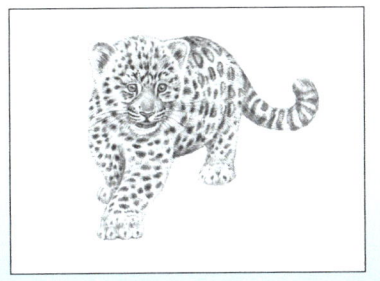
Amur Leopard 1

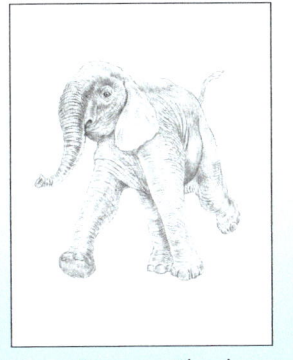
Borneo Pygmy Elephant 4

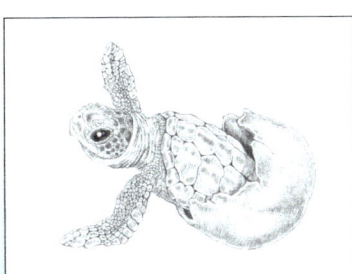
Green Sea Turtle 7

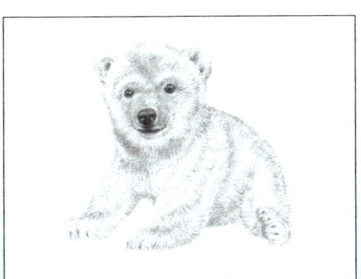
Polar Bear 10

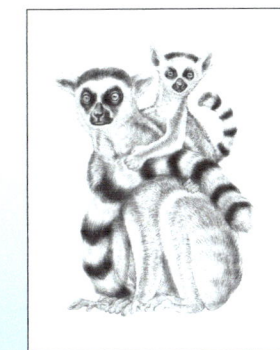
Ring-Tailed Lemurs 13

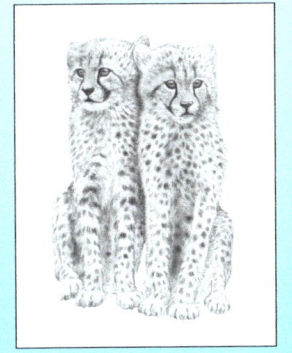
Asiatic Cheetahs 2

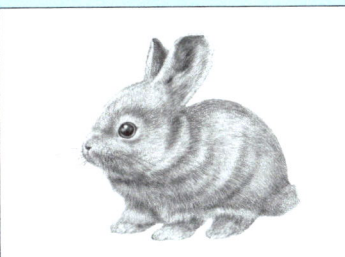
Columbia Basin Pygmy Rabbit 5

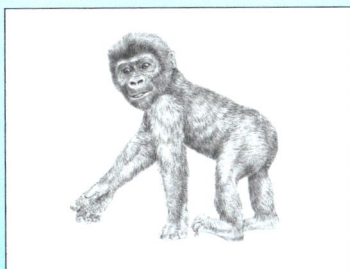
Mountain Gorilla 8

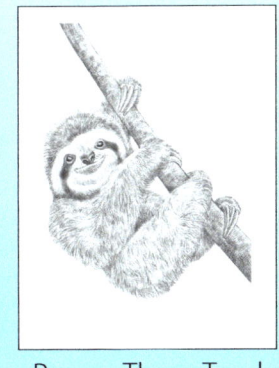
Pygmy Three-Toed Sloth 11

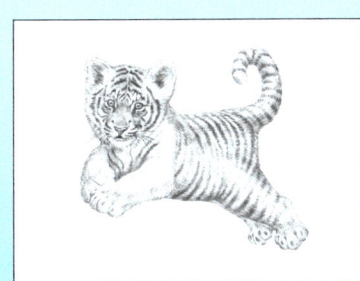
South China Tiger 14

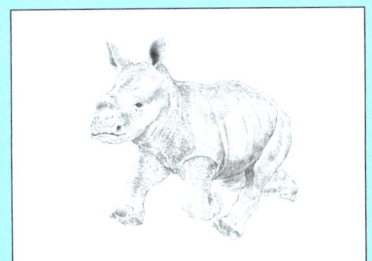
Black Rhinoceros 3

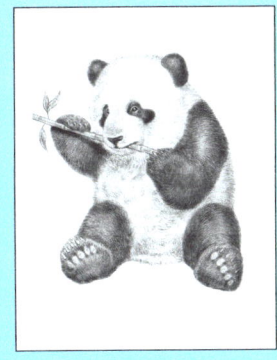
Giant Panda 6

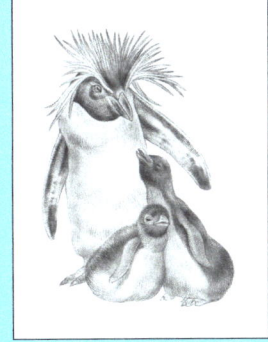
Northern Rockhopper Penguins 9

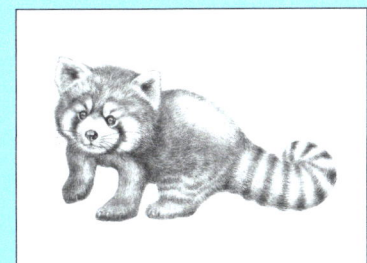
Red Panda 12

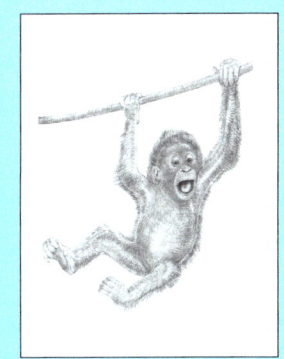
Sumatran Orangutan 15

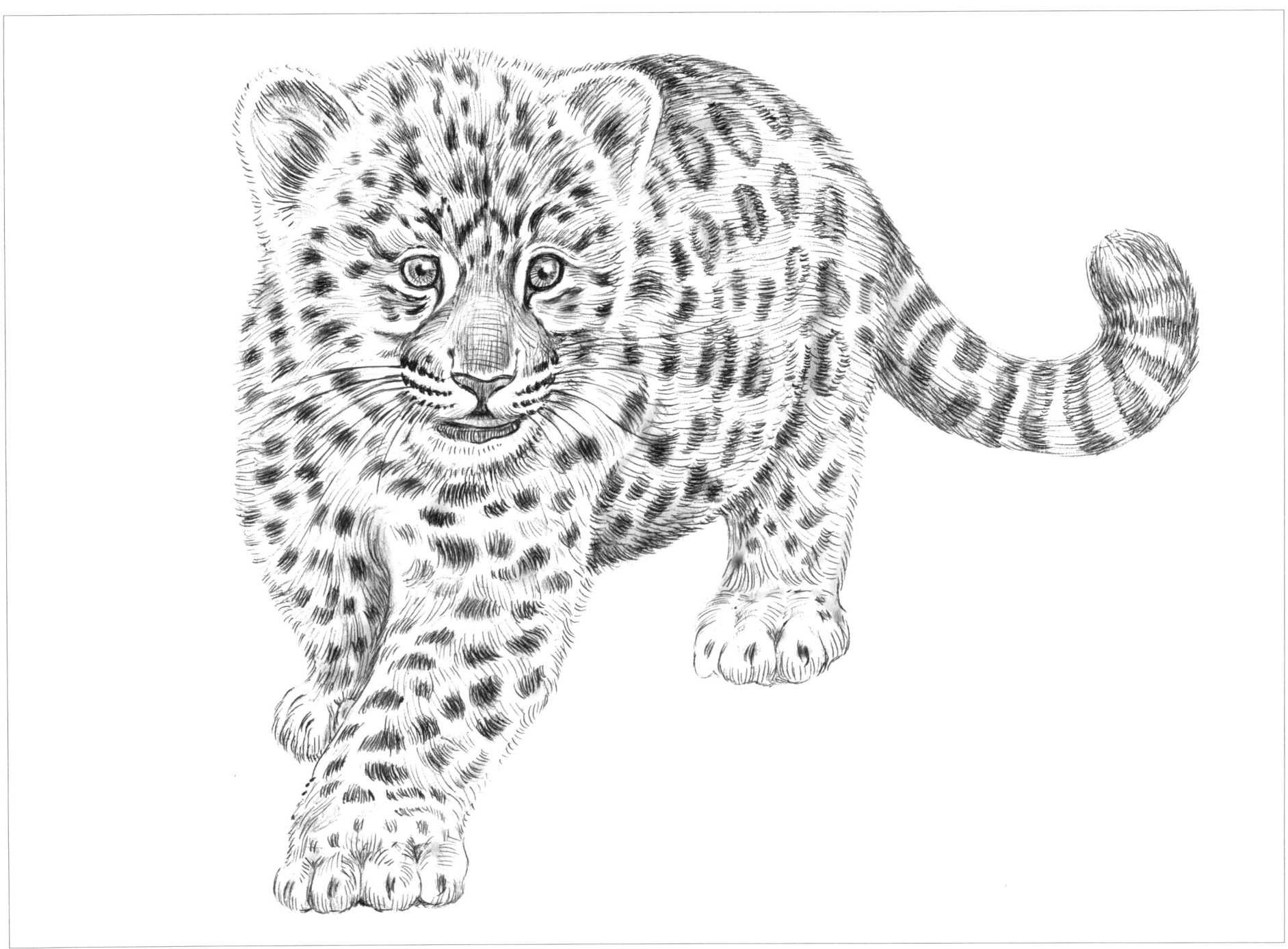

Amur Leopard

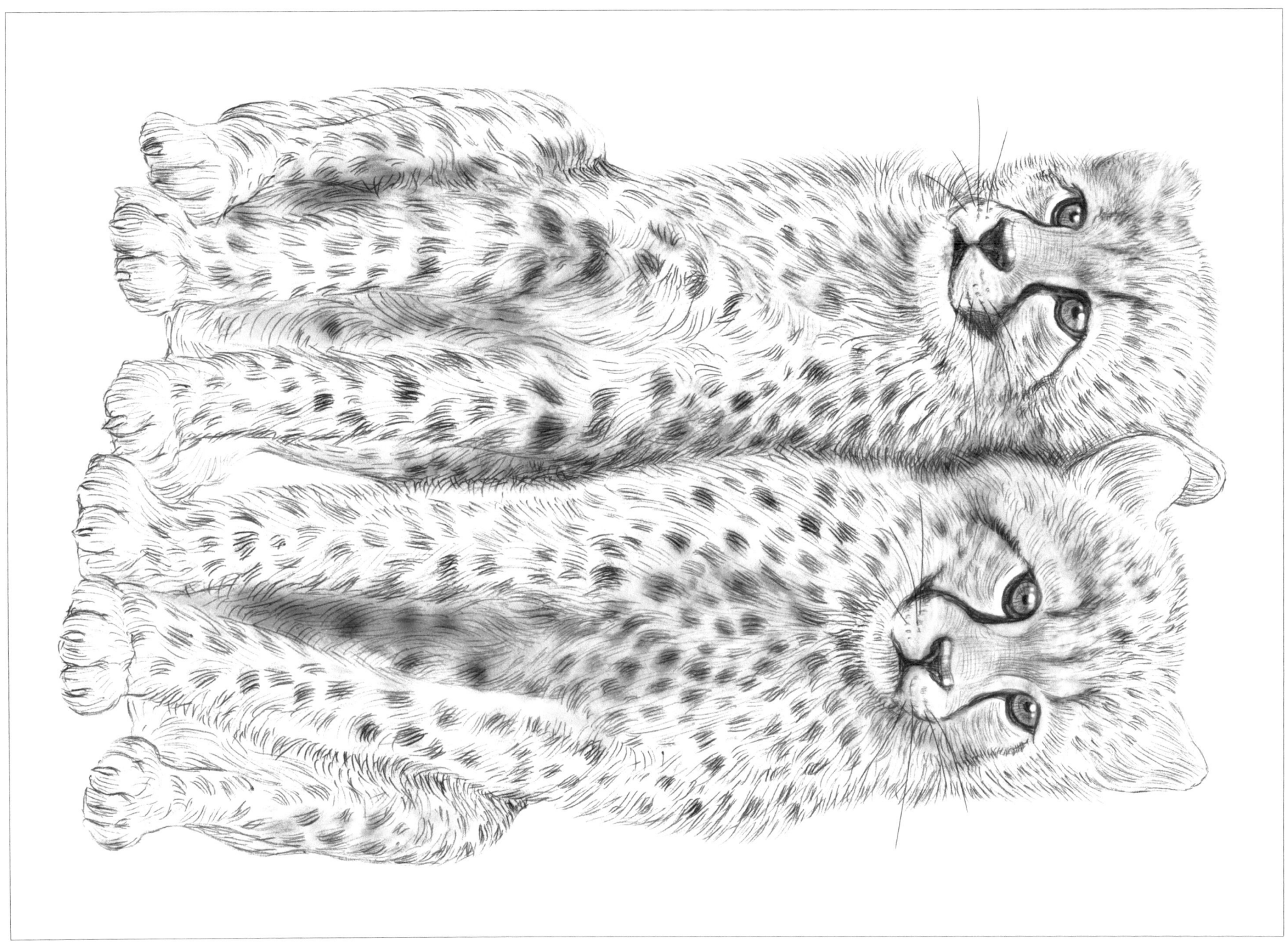

Asiatic Cheetah

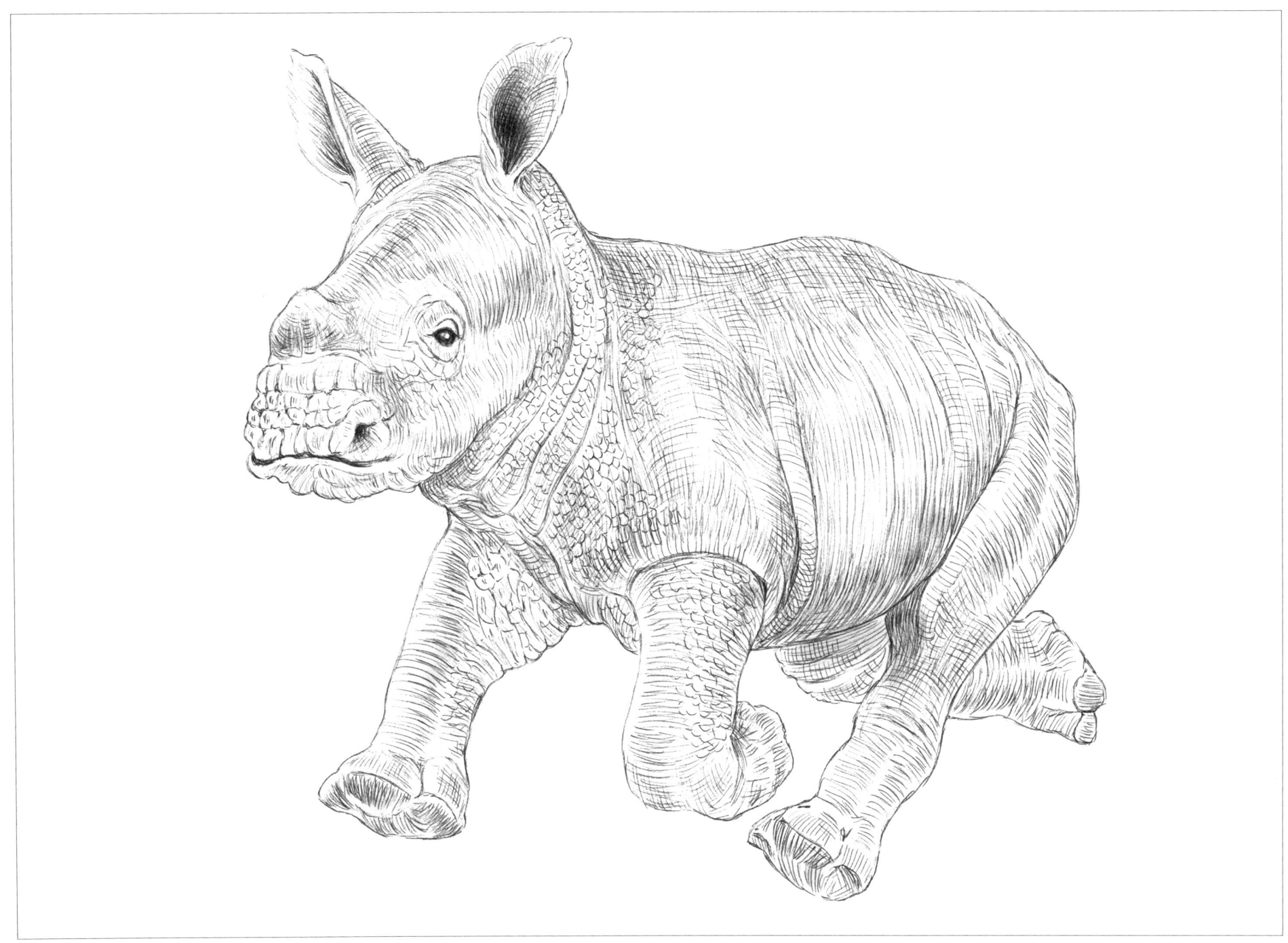

Black Rhinoceros

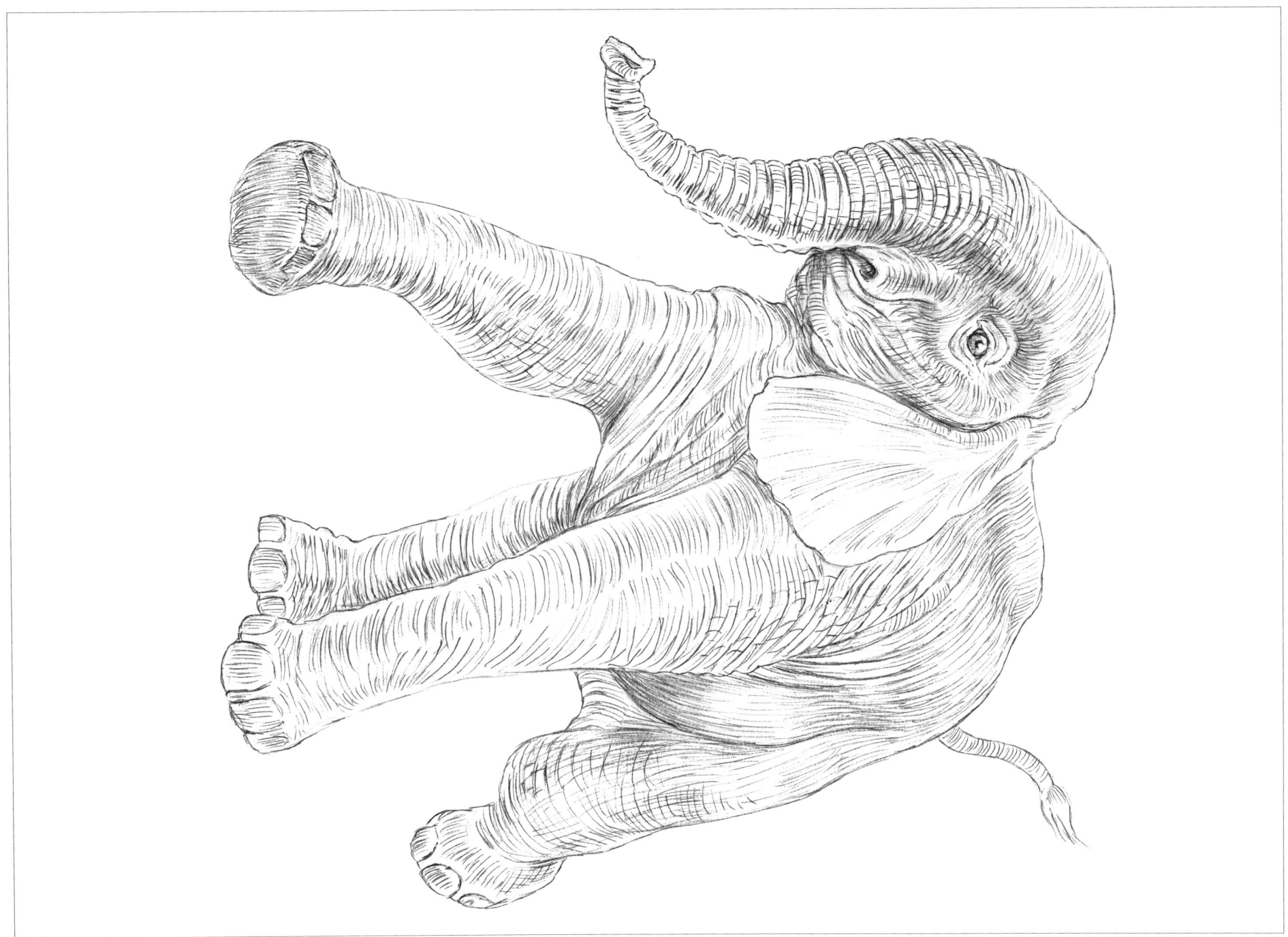

Borneo Pygmy Elephant

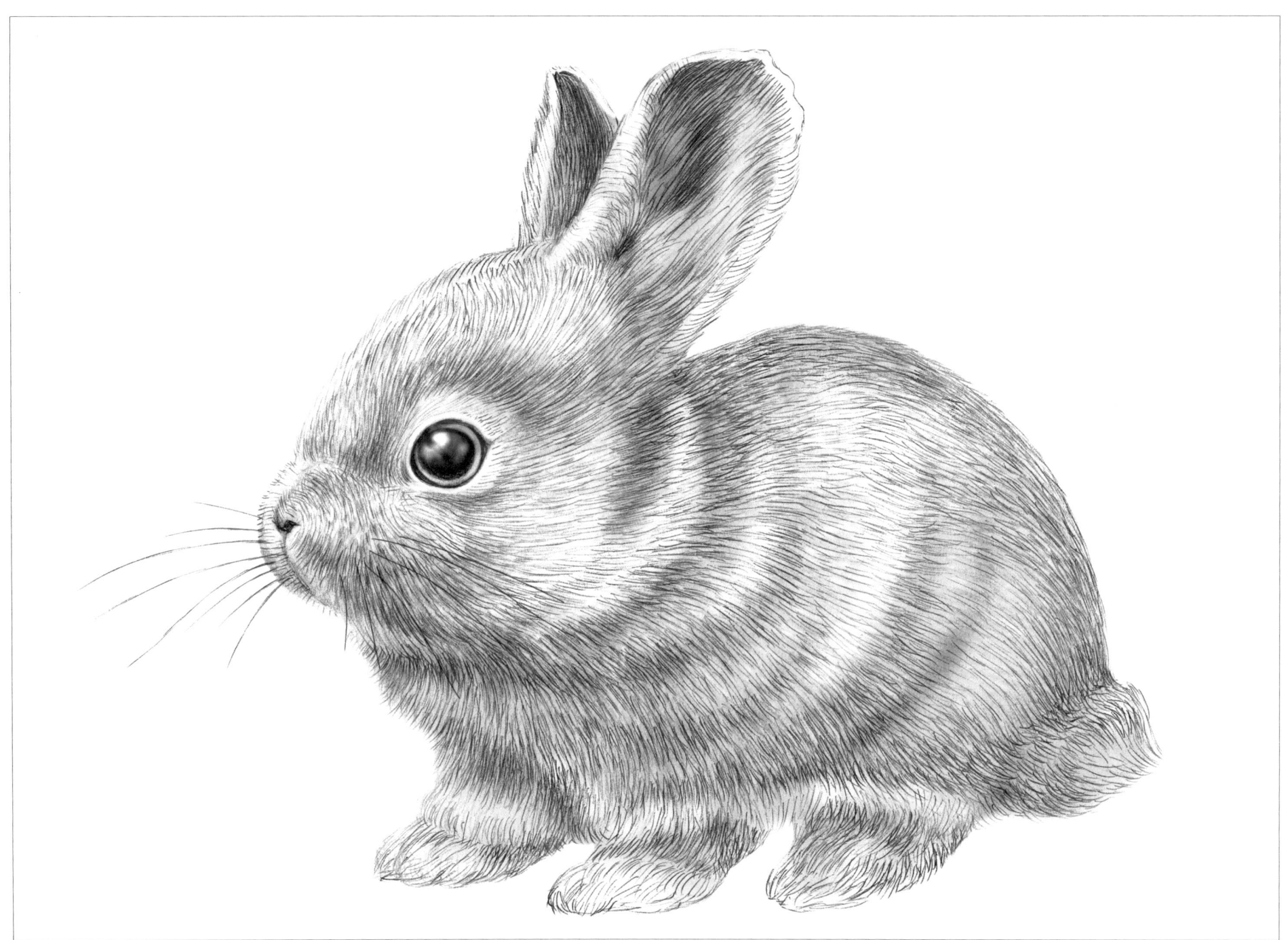

Columbia Basin Pygmy Rabbit

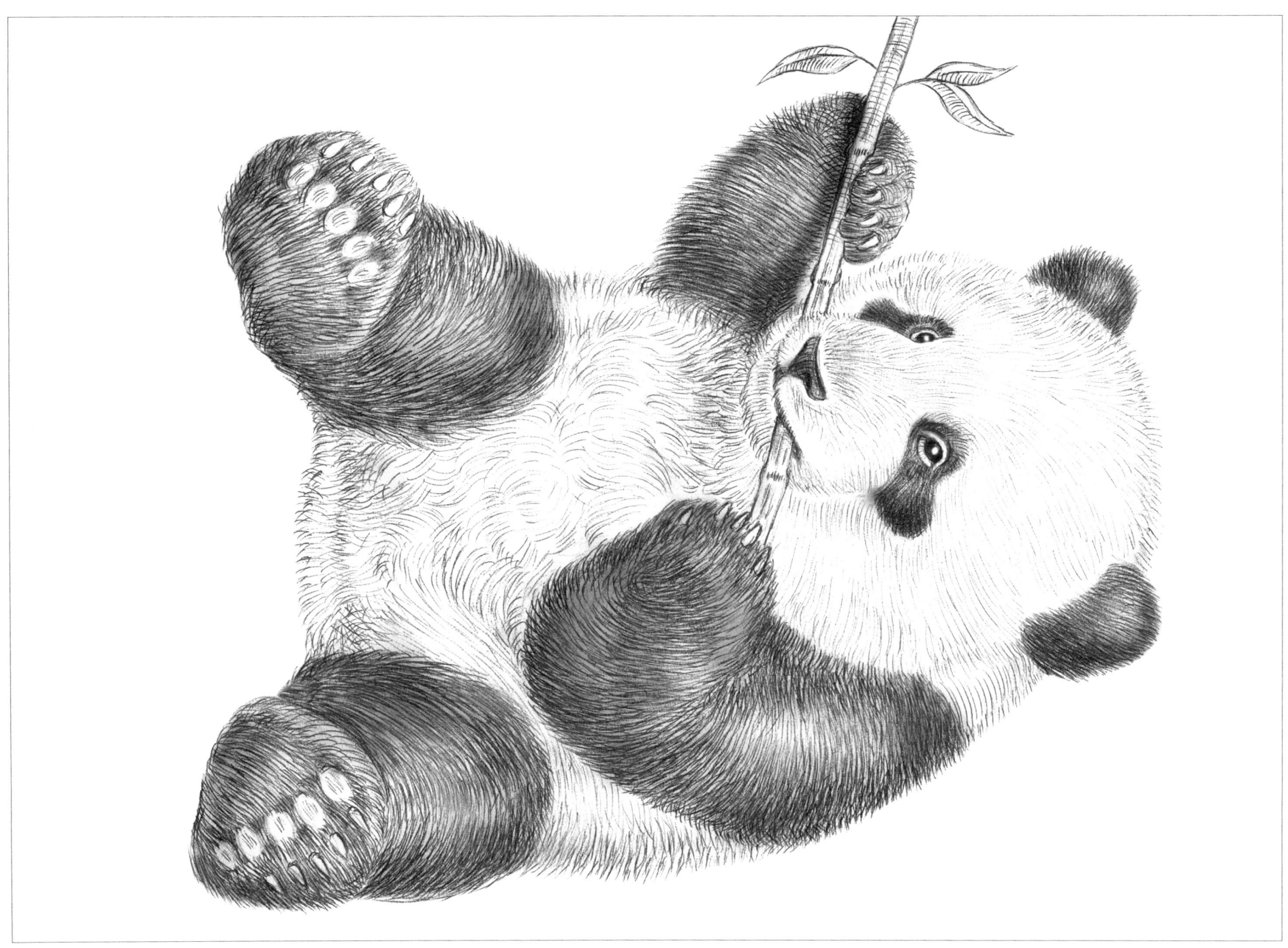

Giant Panda

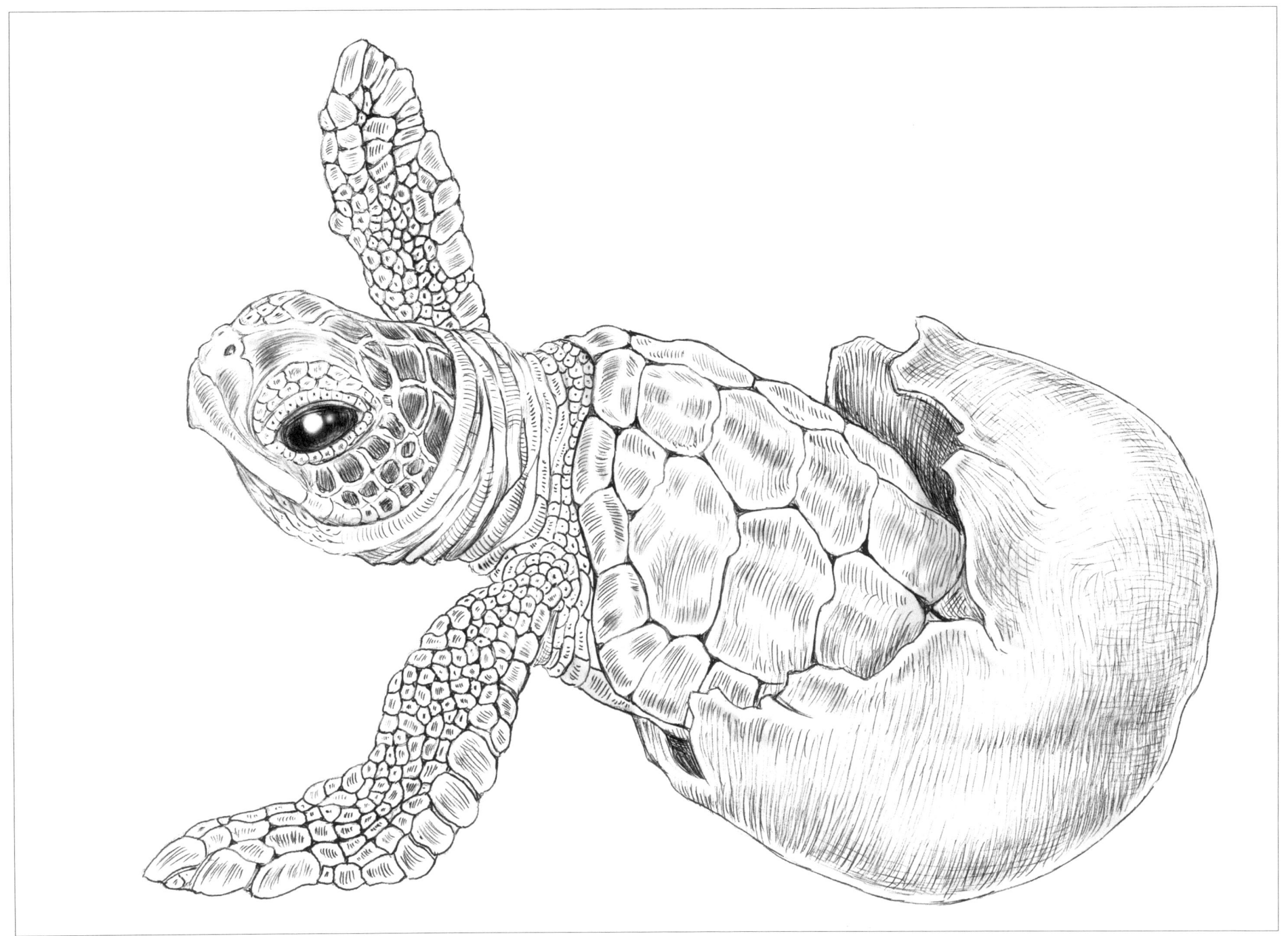

Green Sea Turtle

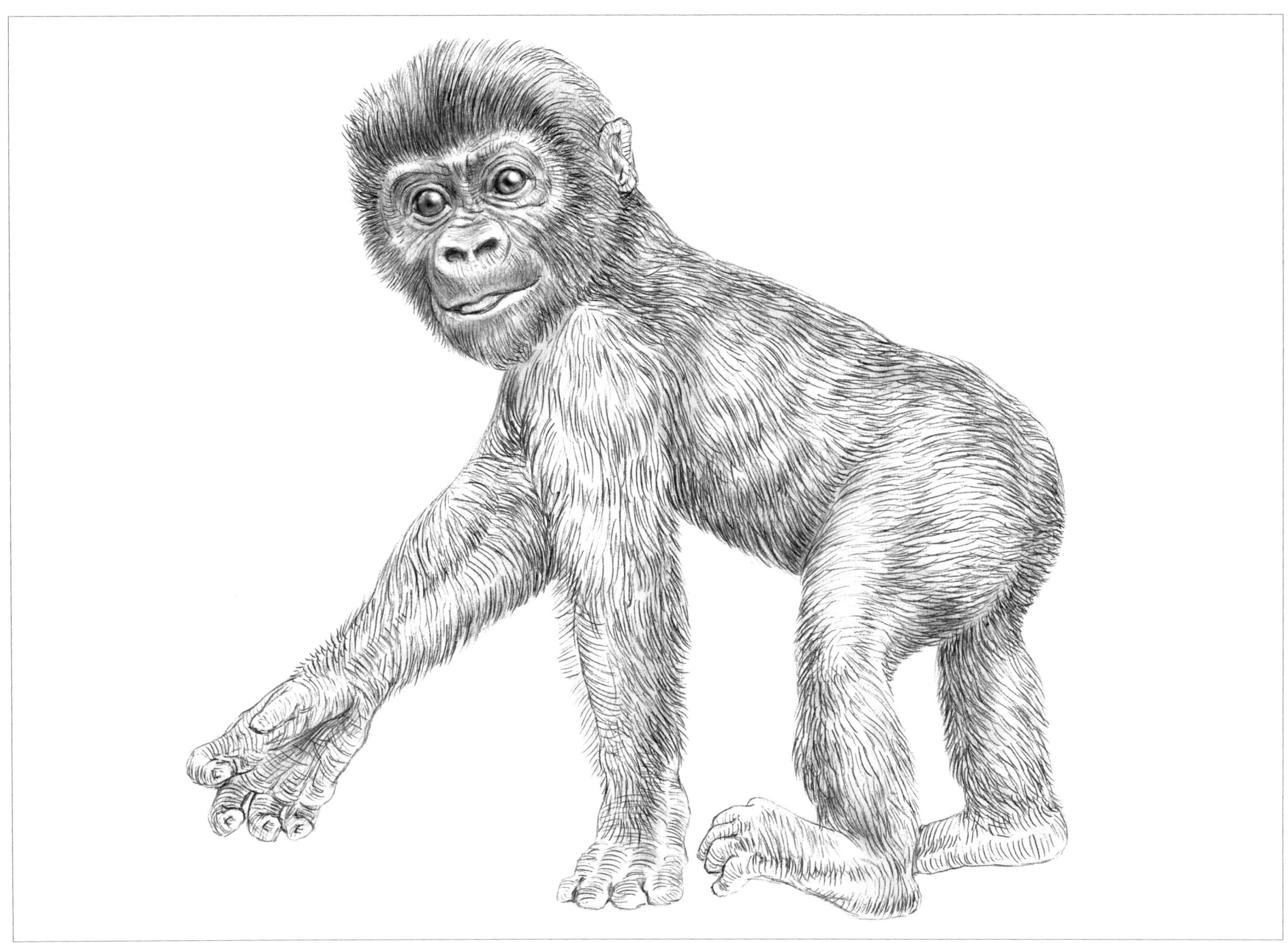

Mountain Gorilla

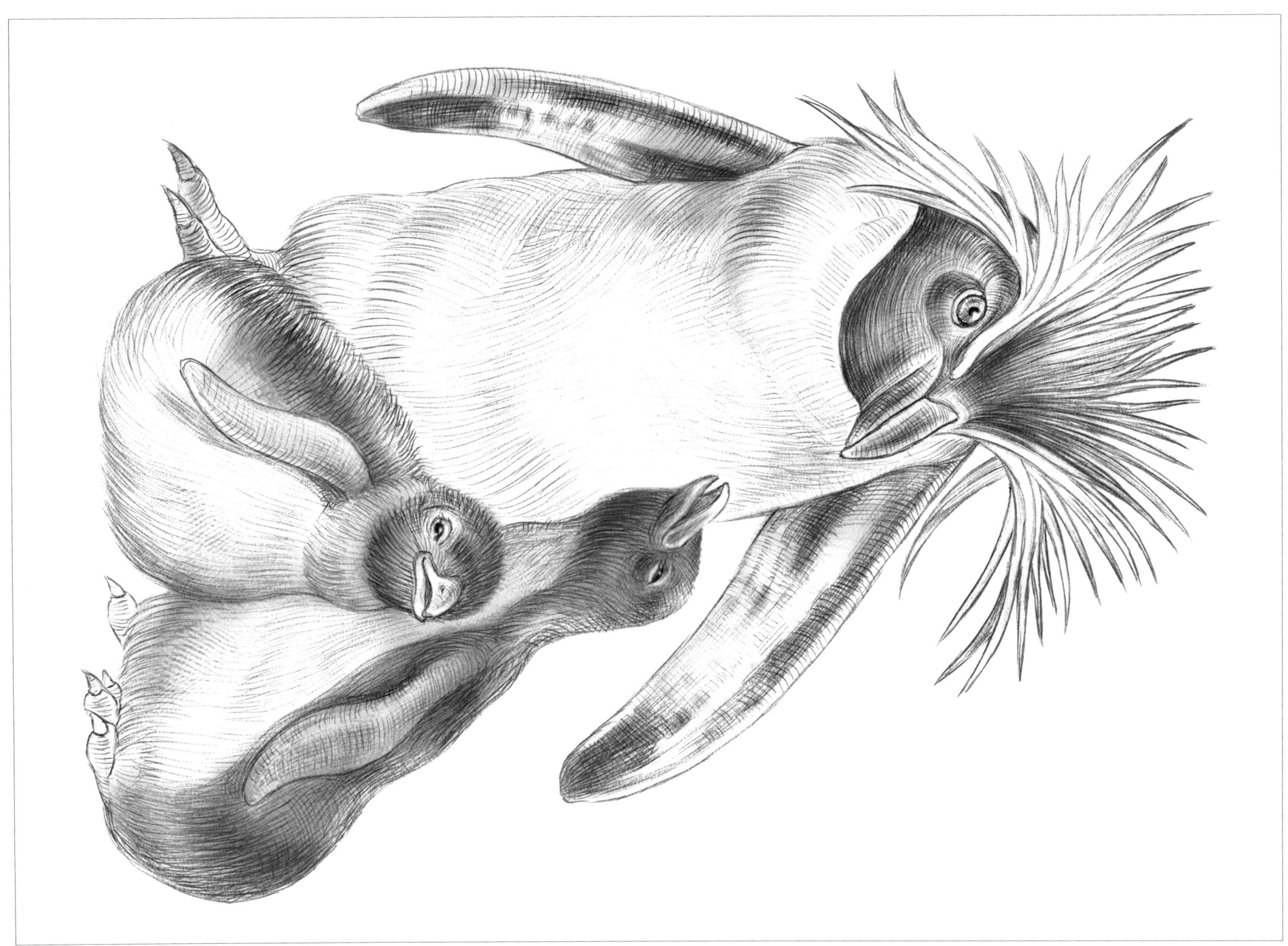

Northern Rockhopper Penguins

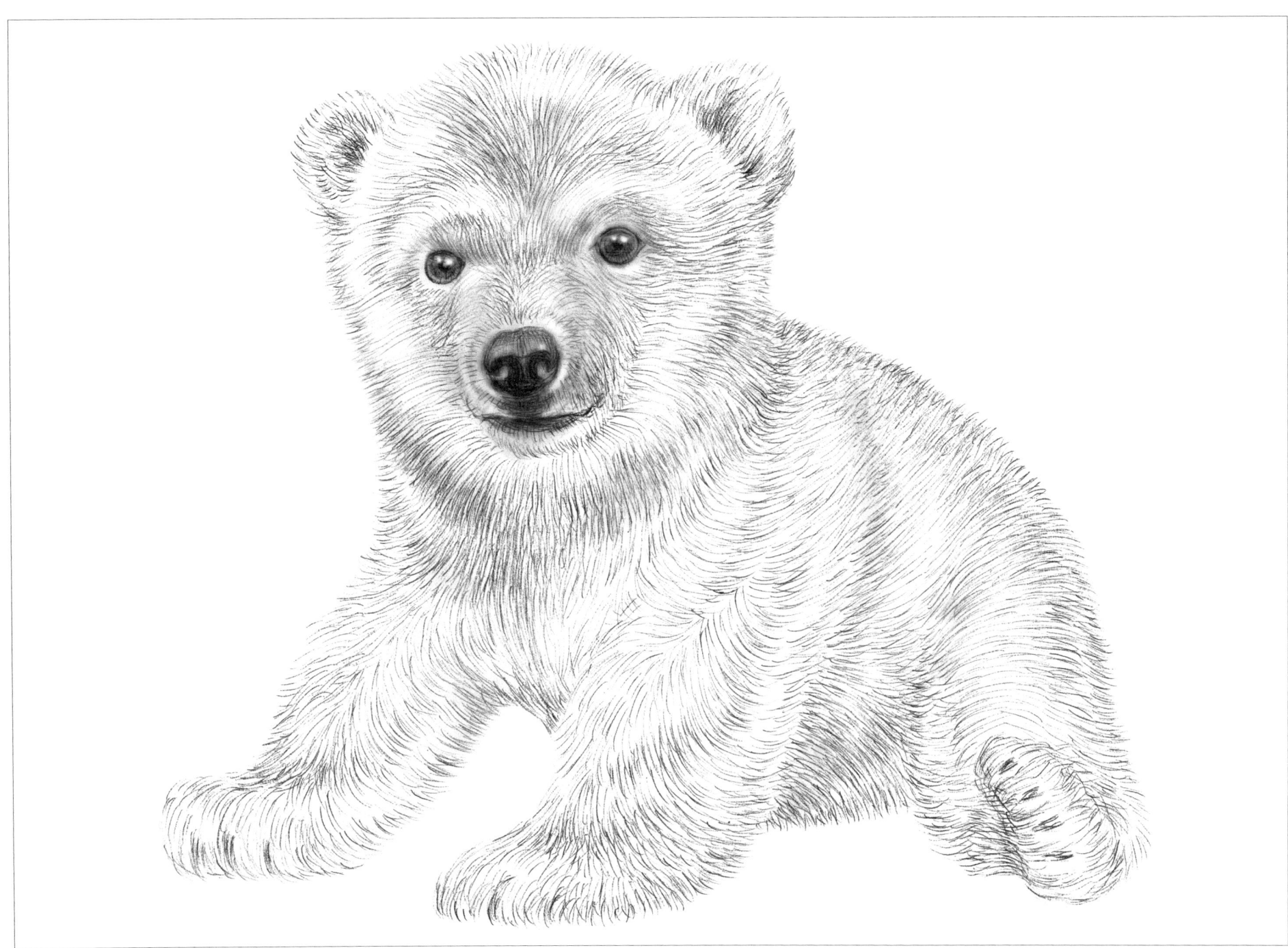

Polar Bear

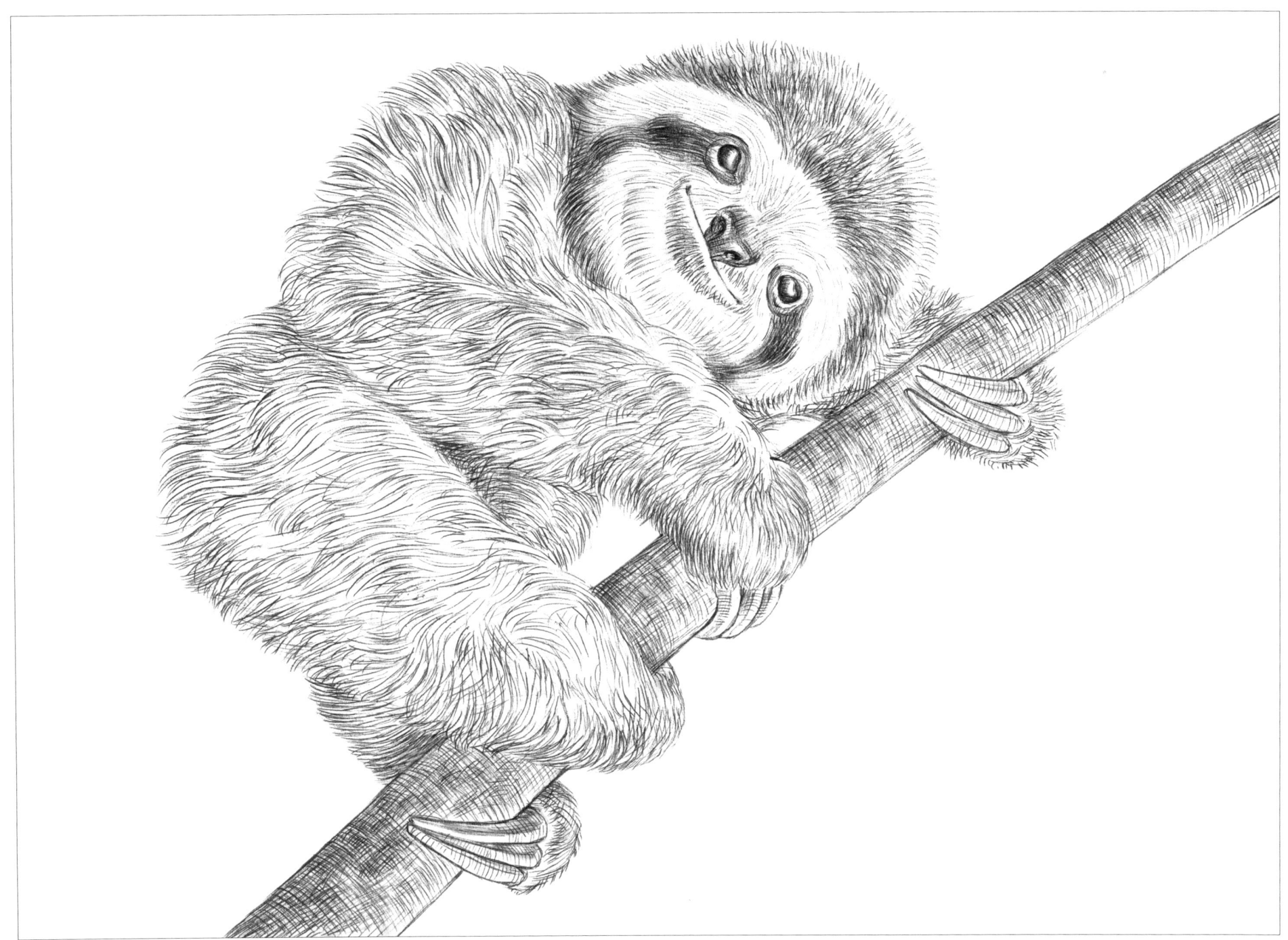

Pygmy Three-Toed Sloth

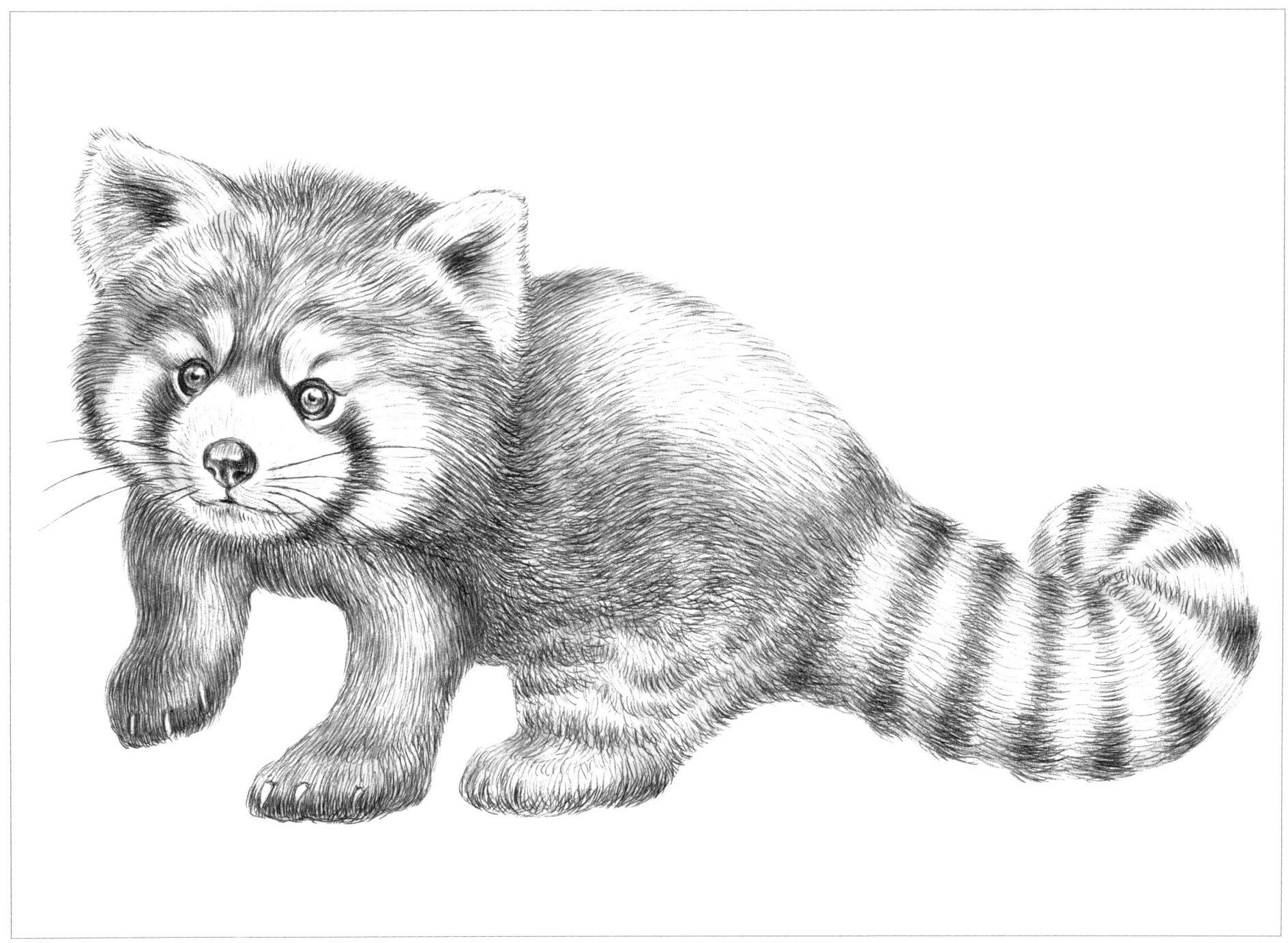

Red Panda

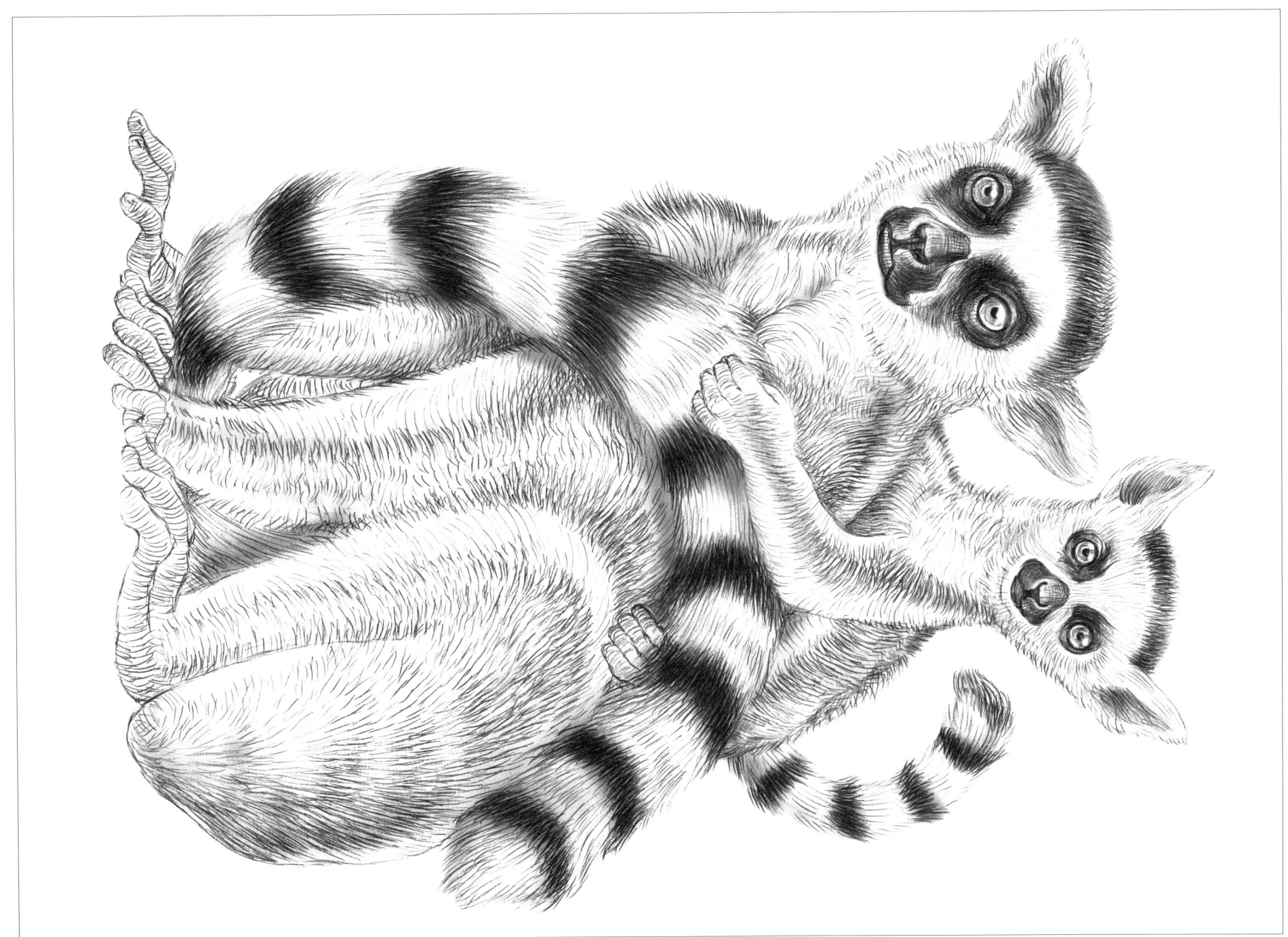

Ring-Tailed Lemurs

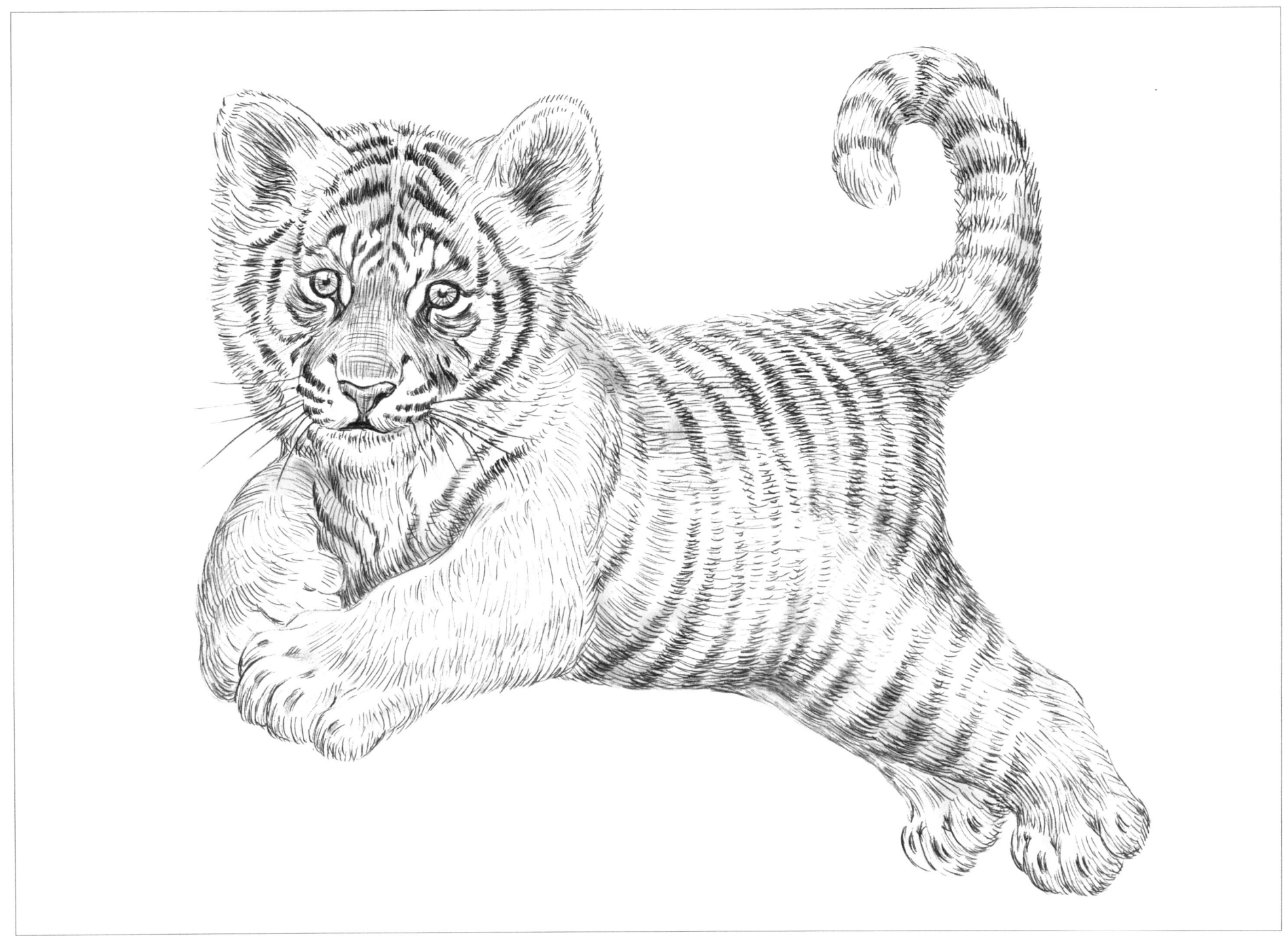

South China Tiger

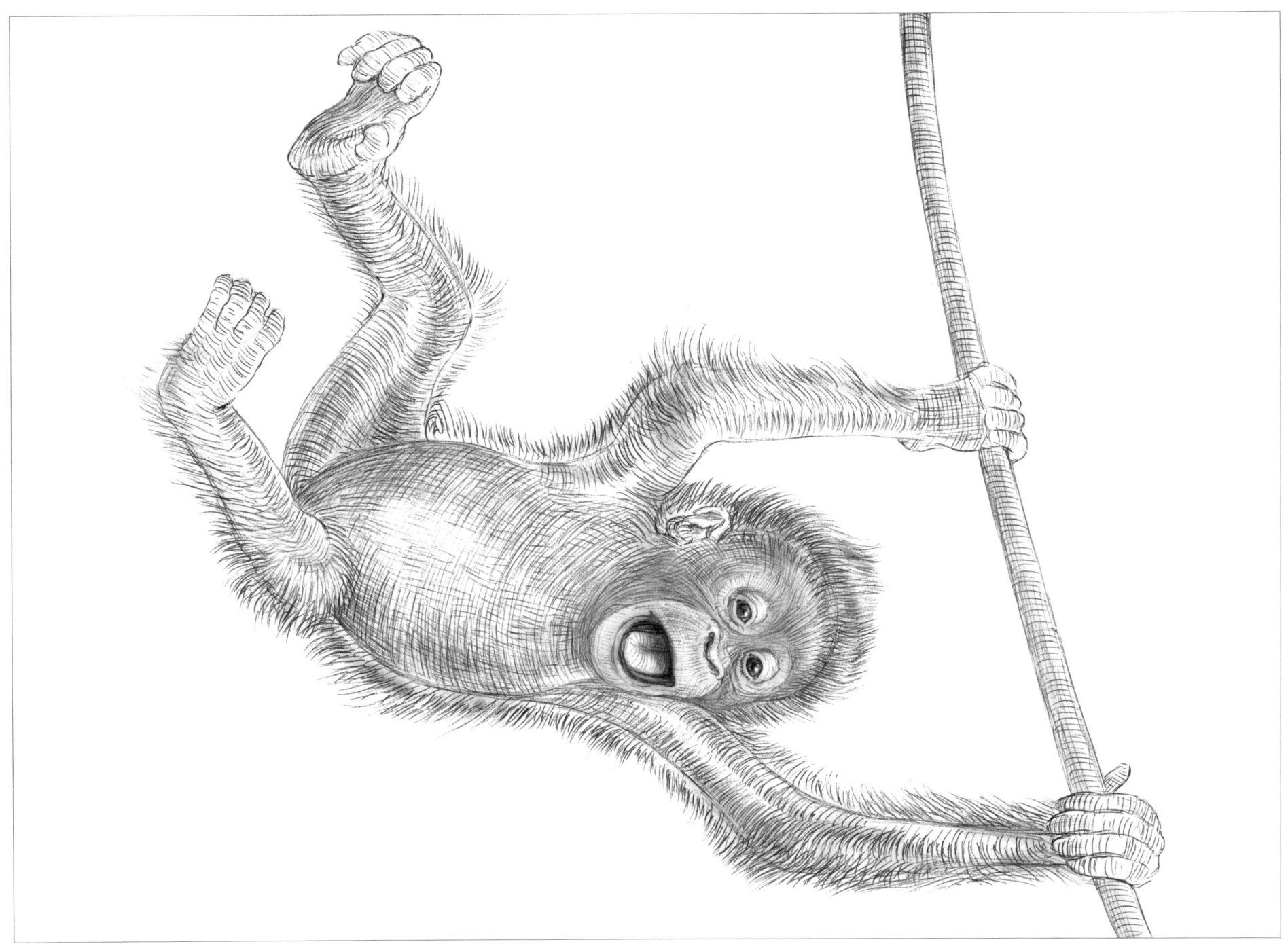

Sumatran Orangutan

Tim Jeffs is a New York City based artist and illustrator who has been creating dynamic artwork for over 25 years. Animals are a favorite subject matter of his, along with the complex and intricate details these creatures possess. *"The incredible diversity and complexity of animals has always intrigued me. They offer endless pleasure to look and marvel upon. In every drawing I try to capture the unique quality of each particular animal. I hope you enjoy my perspective, love and admiration of these incredible creatures."*

Visit my website for prints, digital coloring books and coloring lessons:

www.TimJeffsArt.com

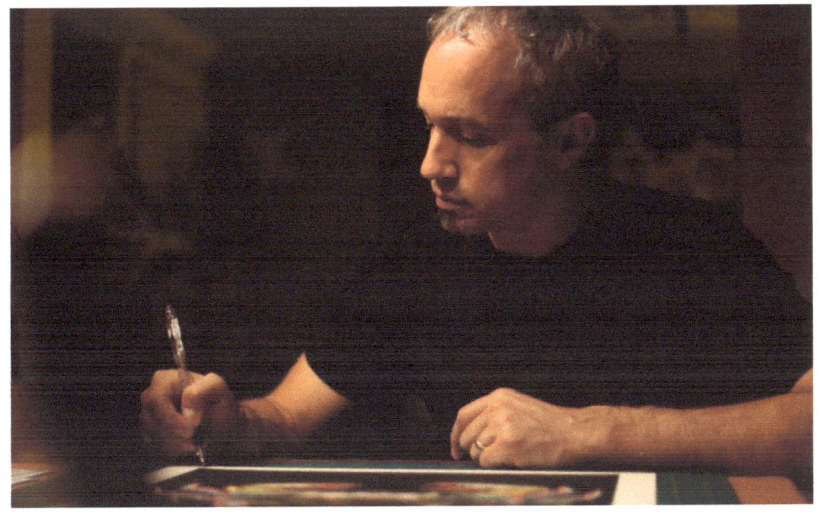

Discover the full line of Tim Jeffs' Published Coloring Books

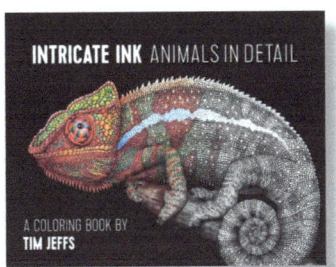 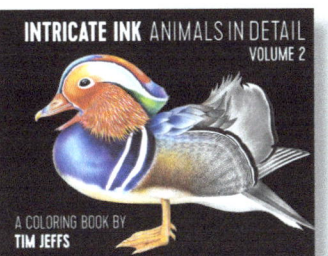 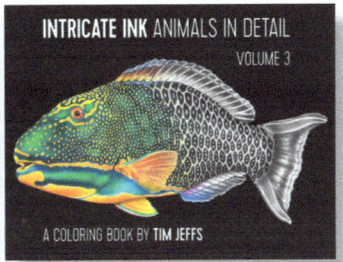 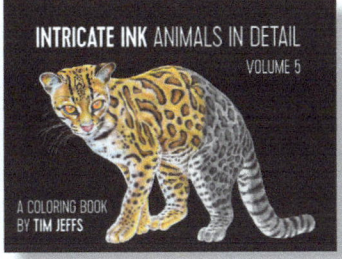 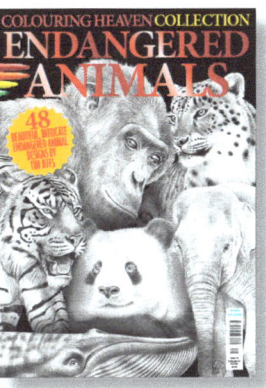

Intricate Ink Animals In Detail Volume 1, 2 3 and 5 Available at:
Pomegranate.com
Amazon.com
Bookdepository.com

**Colouring Heaven Collection
Endangered Animals**
Available at: Colouringheaven.com

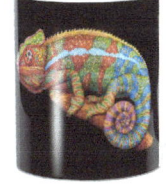

Discover Tim Jeffs' Merchandise

Etsy Shop
www.etsy.com/shop/TimJeffsArt

Society6 Shop
www.society6.com/TimJeffsArt

Redbubble Shop
TimJeffsArt.redbubble.com

Vsual Print Shop
https://vsual.co/shop/tim-jeffs-art

Discover the full line of Tim Jeffs Digital Coloring Books at:
www.TimJeffsArt.com

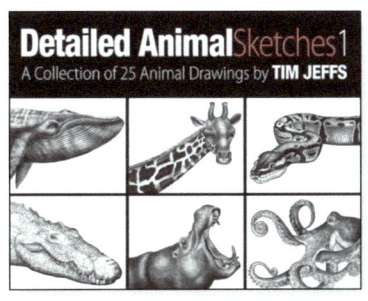
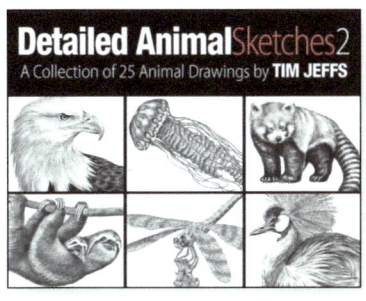
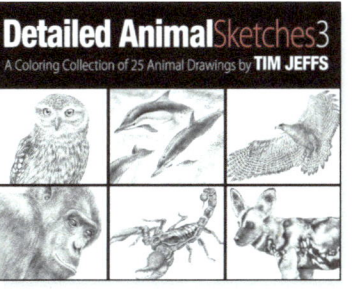
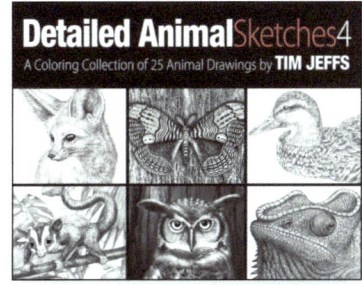
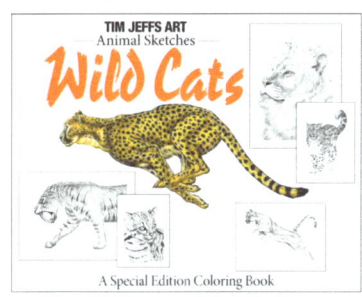
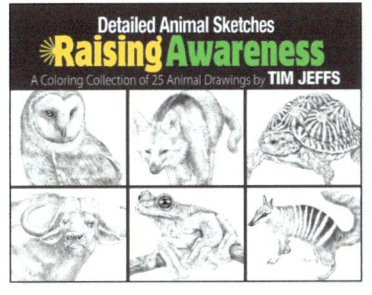
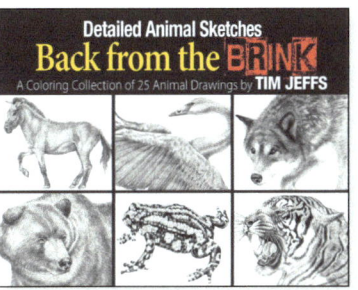
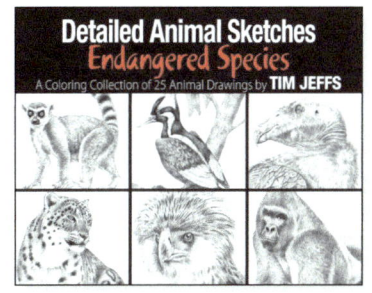
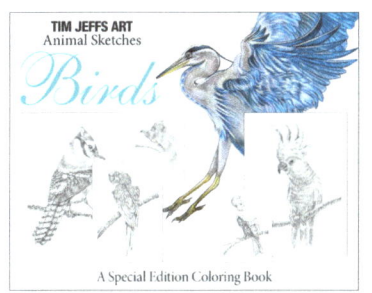
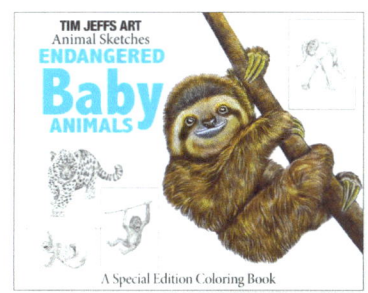

And Coloring Lessons

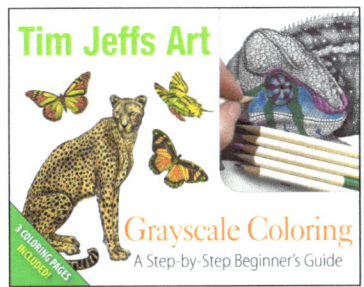
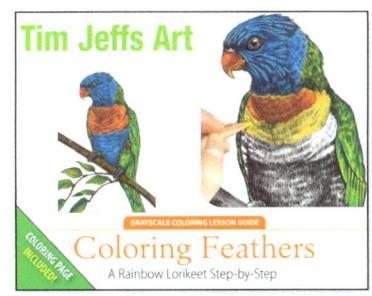
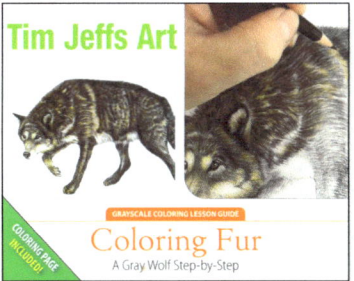
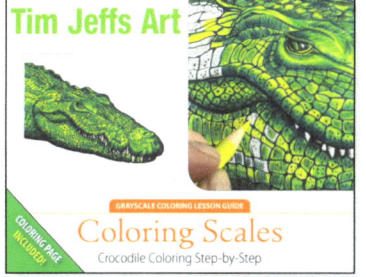
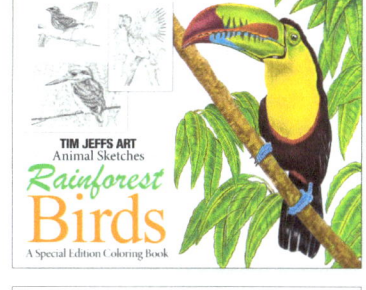
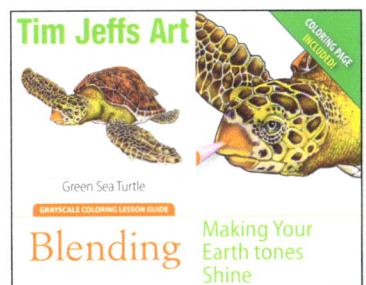
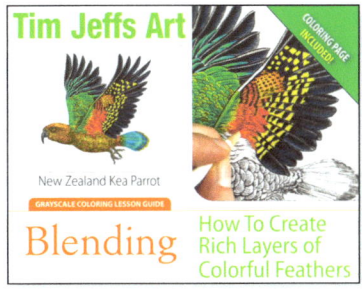
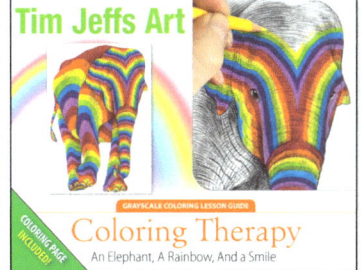
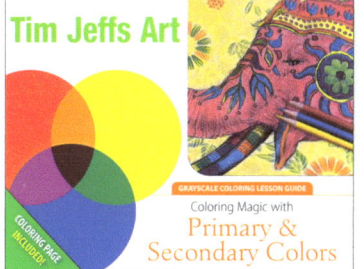
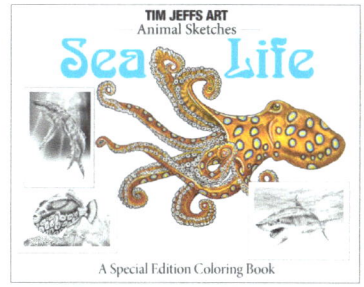

TIM JEFFS ART Online Resources

Share Your Creativity with the World!

Join the ever-expanding coloring group of animal lovers who inspire each other through their colorings of the animals from Tim's books and lessons. With thousands of members from all around the world, Tim's Facebook group "Intricate Ink Coloring Group" is a creative and safe space where everyone is welcome. Jo Warren, the groups all-inspiring administrator will welcome you in with open arms and is there to encourage everyone to just have fun no matter your coloring skill level. Come join, we can't wait to have you as a member! Join Tim's Facebook Coloring Group at:

www.facebook.com/groups/intricateink

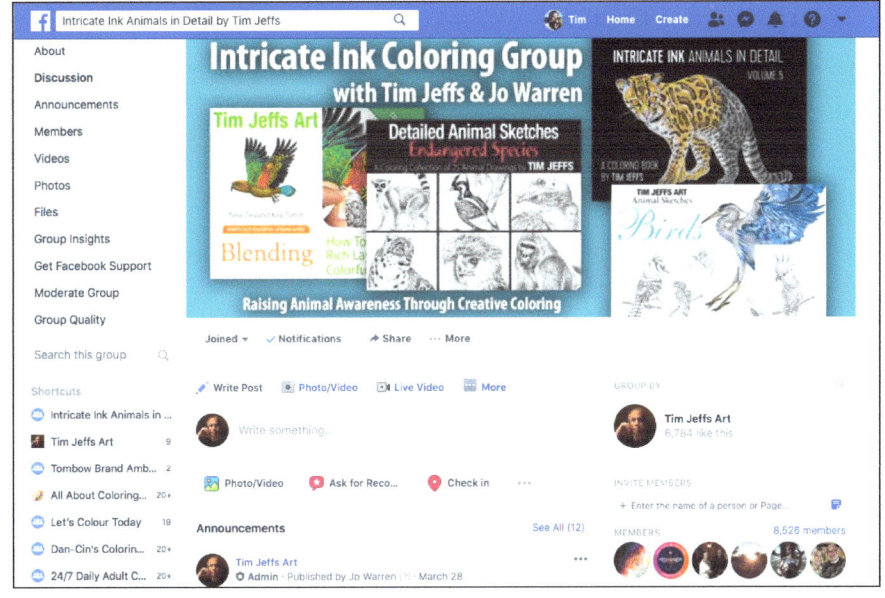

Visit the Home of Tim Jeffs Art

TimJeffsArt.com is my home on the web where I display all of my work and various projects. I hope you can stop by for a visit! You'll find my new shop where signed and unsigned prints of all of my animal drawings are available to purchase, along with the complete library of my digital download coloring books and grayscale coloring lessons. In the conservation section, you can see the projects that I am very proud of. Using my art to preserve wildlife is so important to me.

www.TimJeffsArt.com

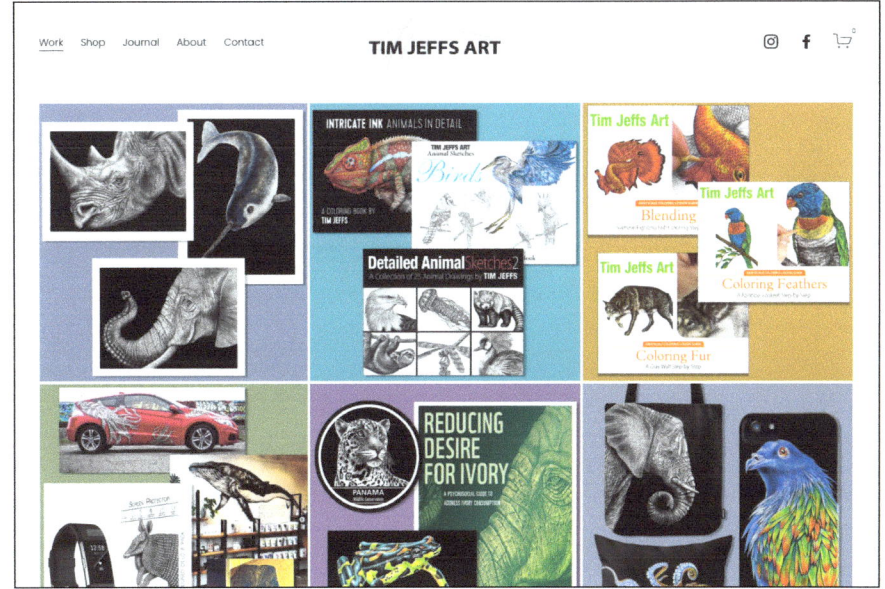